GOD'S SILENCE

GOD'S SILENCE

Poems by

FRANZ WRIGHT

Alfred A. Knopf   New York   2006

THIS IS A BORZOI BOOK
PUBLISHED BY ALFRED A. KNOPF

www.randomhouse.com/knopf/poetry

Knopf, Borzoi Books, and the colophon are registered trademarks of
Random House, Inc.

Library of Congress Cataloging-in-Publication Data
Wright, Franz, [date]
God's silence/Franz Wright.—1st ed.
p. cm.
ISBN 1-4000-4351-4
I. Title.

PS3573.R5327G63 2006
811'.54—dc22   2005051036

Manufactured in the United States of America
First Edition

For Elizabeth, always

Paradise may be the time when we can finally turn to our past and see that its beauty was there despite our being there. In fact, its beauty can finally be seen because we aren't there.

—FANNY HOWE

Is escape . . . too difficult? Evidently, for (1) the walls are strong and I am weak, and (2) I love my walls . . . yet some have escaped. . . . With an effort we lift our gaze from the walls upward and ask God to take the walls away. We look back down and they have disappeared. . . . We turn back upward at once with love to the Person who has made us so happy, and desire to serve Him. Our state of mind is that of a bridegroom, that of a bride. We are married, who have been so lonely heretofore.

—JOHN BERRYMAN

When Moses conversed with God, he asked, "Lord, where shall I seek You?"
God answered, "Among the brokenhearted."
Moses continued, "But, Lord, no heart could be more despairing than mine."
And God replied, "Then I am where you are."

—ABU'L FAYD AL-MISRI

CONTENTS

III

I

EAST BOSTON, 1996

I

ARMED CONFLICT

Snowy light fills the room
pronouncing itself

softly. The telephone ringing

in the deserted city—

ON THE BUS

It's one thing when you're twenty-one,
and I was way past twenty-one.
With unshaven face half concealed in the collar
of some deceased porcine philanthropist's
black cashmere rag of a coat,
I knew that I looked like a suicide
returning an overdue book to the library.
Almost everyone else did as well,
but I found no particular solace in this;
at best, the fact awakened some diverting speculations
on the comparative benefits
of waiting in front of a ditch to be shot
alone or in company

3

of others, and then whether one would prefer
these last hypothetical others
to be friends, family, enemies, total
or relative strangers. Would you hold hands?
Or would you rather like a good *Homo sapiens*
monster employ them
to cover your genitals?
What percentage would lose bowel control?
And given time restrictions—
and assuming some still had the ability to move—
would ostracism result? Anyway,
I knew the rules on this bus.
No eye contact: the eyes of the terrified
terrify. Look
like you know where you're going,
possess ample change to get there,
and don't move your lips when you talk
to yourself: the destroyed
and sick, the poor, the hungry
and the disturbed estrange.
The badly dressed estrange, even,
and that is uncalled for. The degree
of one's power to estrange will increase
in direct proportion to the depth
of need for others. Do not cry.
This can only bring about, on the one hand,
an instant condition of banishment
from the sole available companionship, or
on the other, a near
fatal beating (one more disappointment).
Just follow the simple instruction
if you ever come here.

It's easy to remember—any idiot can do it.
Don't cry,
the world has abandoned us.

NIGHT WALK

The all-night convenience store's empty
and no one is behind the counter.
You open and shut the glass door a few times
causing a bell to go off,
but no one appears. You only came
to buy a pack of cigarettes, maybe
a copy of yesterday's newspaper—
finally you take one and leave
thirty-five cents in its place.
It is freezing, but it is a good thing
to step outside again:
you can feel less alone in the night,
with lights on here and there
between the dark buildings and trees.
Your own among them, somewhere.
There must be thousands of people
in this city who are dying
to welcome you into their small bolted rooms,
to sit you down and tell you
what has happened to their lives.
And the night smells like snow.
Walking home, for a moment
you almost believe you could start again.
And an intense love rushes to your heart,
and hope. It's unendurable, unendurable.

In a clearing in the cornstalks, in light
November snow it was suggested
that I fire
on that muttering family of crows.
I complied
and watched as those big ruffled shadows
rose from the ground, scattered and vanished
in the direction of barren
border trees, commencing
to speak all at once
in hysterical tongues.
All except for one,
deceased.
I turned it over with my boot.
The eyes stared
at the sky, the minute
snowflakes falling into them.
Its beak was partly opened.
It was then I vomited a little.
This achievement was the last thing I'd expected
when they dug up the old .22
for my afternoon's amusement
and banishment. I was just eight, but I swore
then and there
my career as death was finished.
The ground was hard but I considered
going back to the house for a shovel;
it did not seem wholly implausible
that I might turn around to find

my victim limping after me,
and I ended up walking away from the house
for an hour or so.
Later on I cried and told my mother.
She comforted me, as I knew perfectly well she would.
In her opinion I was not to blame.
It was that gun. And besides,
she was certain crows had their own heaven.
I was off the hook.
My crow was much better off now.
That's what she thought.

HOME REMEDY

You could call someone
where it's still early.

Go out and look at the stars
shining
in the past.

Or open the Joachim Jeremias to the densely printed
page, its corner folded
for some reason
not yet remembered

before you set the clock.

You have to set the clock—
for a moment that doesn't exist yet

or one that has already passed, interestingly
symbolized by the identical numeral.

The friendly medications are beginning
to kick in: the frightening
objects
emitting the faint nimbus
of their reality, slowly
returning
to normal,

if this had been an actual emergency.

íi

The long silences need to be loved, perhaps
more than the words
which arrive
to describe them
in time.

REPARATIONS

The day's coming
when I will no longer consider
my mere presence inexpiable.
I will place my hand in that flame
and feel nothing.

8

I will ask nobody's forgiveness again.
Or I will just go
among people no more—
I may writhe with
remorse in the night, but
the operation must be
undertaken by
me, anesthesialess.
No one must be asked to relinquish
a grievance that can't be removed
without further destruction, it may be
it is lodged in who he is now
like a bullet in a brain
whose removal might just cause worse change.
The forgiveness! I know it
will be freely offered
or it won't, and that is all—
and no one may bestow it
on himself.
If it is to come
it will come of itself like a separate
being,
a mystery, working
unseen as a wind causes still
leaves or water to move once again.
And hide me in the shadow of Your wings.

Let the heart be moved again.

II

BEGINNING AGAIN

"If I could stop talking, completely
cease talking for a year, I might begin
to get well," he muttered.
Off alone again performing
brain surgery on himself
in a small badly lit
room with no mirror. A room
whose floor, ceiling and walls
are all mirrors, what a mess
oh my God—

And still
it stands,
the question
not how begin
again, but rather

Why?

So we sit there
together
the mountain
and me, Li Po
said, until only the mountain
remains.

THE TWO

They were standing there
above me when I woke
Franz I heard them say
in unison though neither's lips moved

and there was no sound
no interruption
of the silence I heard
the word in my mind

as if I had imagined it
or spoken it aloud
myself
but the voice was not mine

the voices I should say
then like sunlight
when a cloud obscures the sun suddenly
they were gone.

TRANSFORMATION

It gets late early now
This is
when I like to visit
you at the top of your hidden
still green stairway, holy
Mother with the downcast
eyes as a girl of sixteen
almost unnoticed the right bare foot pinning
the serpent with the one-
leafed little apple in its jaws
poor thing, one is tempted
to say, so transformed
by its contact with you
is everything—

PROGRESS

Nobody has called for some time.
(I was always the death of the party.)

In a way that leaves
a scar, I
no longer wish to love.

(Come a hairbreadth closer
to this shining
apparition and be consumed in flame.)

I'm still alone with all the world's
beauty and cruelty.

And I recall
everything,
everything's
here—
what is time? When
is the present?

I'm still here alone in the night hours with everyone.

And everything that once was
infinitely far
and unsayable is now
unsayable
and right here in the room.

FROM THE PAST

I suffer from insomnia, from loneliness I sleep. From the past I suffer, and the imminence of some radiantly obvious thing I need to say, though quite what that might be escapes me at the moment, as it always has, and always will. And I can just see it: I'll be driven to the hospital for the last time with my toothbrush and razor at about two in the afternoon, the turnpike deserted, the lights of some new isolated office building beckoning celestially on a distant hill. "It smells like snow," I will say. I'm saying. I said.

But who was *I*, so clearly it appeared to me that there was something else than what I saw? Who did I imagine I was, that things as they are, reality as God gave it, was not enough for me?

THE VISITING

I suffer from insomnia, from loneliness I sleep;
in the midst of the talk and the laughter
all at once you are there—

Hour of waking up and writhing
with humiliation, or
of wishes answered before

one was aware of what they were.
And let me ask you this: the dead,
where *aren't* they?

Hour when the ones who can't rest
go to bed, and the ones
who can't wake go to work—

Dark blue morning glory
I reach to touch, there is another world
and it is this world.

Then the light streamed in yellow
and blue through long windows, and blood
turned to wine in my veins.

Tears of wine
rode down my cheek.
It's happening, I thought,

though it had never happened
before. I squeezed
my eyes closed, gazing into

a darkness all of light. The more
you tried to hold it back, the more
sweetly and irresistibly it arrived.

THE TRUTH WILL SET YOU FREE

You are the lamp, and you are the night.
This small upstairs window is yours
to look out from, this cot is
for your exhaustion alone; this single
drop of water's going to cure your thirst forever!
And these four walls belong to the being
your pure light brought into the world,
oh prisoner—

oh bride.

Translated from the French of René Char

EMPEROR OF ANTARCTICA

What is that, a blizzard
or a soundless
pavane?

Everyone treats me so nicely here
I think I must be dead.

No longer a boy
afraid of the dark, but a man
terrified
of the
light
suddenly flooding his room every day.

Light of earth,
visible sacrament
of God's awareness. Light
of the far unvisitable
peaks, the
light the corpse's face
seems bathed in
or emits—

DID THIS EVER HAPPEN TO YOU

A marble-colored cloud
engulfed the sun and stalled,

a skinny squirrel limped toward me
as I crossed the empty park

and froze, the last
or next to last

fall leaf fell but before it touched
the earth, with shocking clarity

I heard my mother's voice
pronounce my name. And in an instant I passed

beyond sorrow and terror, and was carried up
into the imageless

bright darkness
I came from

and am. Nobody's
stronger than forgiveness.

CHILD PLAYING

Among the other dusty
basement shadows, I

aimlessly amuse myself;
I hear the rain all at once stop

and stop myself, witnessing
a ray of gold dusk enter

through the cracked window—
it stands before me like a stair

or being come, perhaps
to beckon me alone

up stairways you can't see. Something
I already know myself fully prepared

to take her up on, should
the opportunity arrive. How glad

I am, and hum a little
song I like, still

do: I know the words
that go along with it, though, now:

who's had to love the madness
of his loneliness is blessed.

OD HEARING

There are people I know in the room, but
what they have to say
is strange:

      If we were wolves
we'd turn on you
without a second thought

without
a first thought
and move on . . .

I quit.

Let the other
five billion perceive
the universe into existing for one more day.

         Kiss me
an easy death whispers: I want you to
come in my mouth—

        Wolves
with bright amethyst teeth smiling.

ALDER STREET

Alcohol's effect (on *us*):
how was it Lowry described it—
A dead tree struck by lightning
which thereupon miraculously
blossoms.

And what then? Always,
always comes the
then what:
            I speak of

the Fear.

Too well what I refer to one of you will understand!

Having one of your own, too well you know
the idiot I have to babysit
to keep him from sleepwalking off
to a package store somewhere
or conning some doctor even dumber than he is
into prescribing his death.

*

Someone new may speak
if I, today, keep silent.

And any chair
that's empty here,

that's someone
who is dying:

Find him.

POEM IN TWO PARTS

1. Contributor's Note

My parents (all
four of them) did
their very best, and yet

I did not die.
At nineteen
I received the dark crown—

Of course, it crushed my head
a minor
side effect

a stroke of sorts, but now
I walk again
a little

like a broken doll
but walk
again I talk

and stranger still

this time
you are all listening

2. Parallel Self

It's not my fault
if I was born

without a heart,
I live

in a universe
all light

with stars
of darkness, a hell

of light I married

a deathstyle, my father
whatever

I married

in a sky
blue dress

that once belonged
to Frances Farmer, dreamily

smiling
with an ice pick

in my skull, it
was all

in my mind.

WOODS HOLE FERRY

Crossing briefly this mirrory still Galilean blue water to the heaven
of the affluent, the users-up, unconsciously remote
from knowing themselves
our owners and starvers, occupying
as they always have, to no purpose,
the mansions and the beauty of the earth
for this short while
before
we all meet and enter at the same door.

SITTING UP LATE WITH MY FATHER, 1977

White fire of winter stars—
what he's thinking at fifty
I finally know.

He thinks, so the blizzards will come
and I will be healed;
we'll talk

when you grow up
and I am dead.

White distant emerald fire of winter stars.

PUBLICATION DATE

One of the few pleasures of writing
is the thought of one's book in the hands of a kindhearted
intelligent person somewhere. I can't remember what the others
        are right now.
I just noticed that it is my own private

National I Hate Myself and Want to Die Day
(which means the next day I will love my life
and want to live forever). The forecast calls
for a cold night in Boston all morning

and all afternoon. They say
tomorrow will be just like today,
only different. I'm in the cemetery now
at the edge of town, how did I get here?

A sparrow limps past on its little bone crutch saying
I am Federico García Lorca
risen from the dead—
literature will lose, sunlight will win, don't worry.

FOUR POEMS OF YOUTH

1. The Dream

Later
that now long lost night
in December, beside you, I saw
that the leaves had returned
to the branches
outside my window. Now
that is all it was: leaves, blowing
in the windy sunlight: somehow,
in spite of the chances against it
occurring, in spite of the critic's wan sneer,
I dreamed this gorgeous thing.

2. Minneapolis, 1960

Children in a classroom peer
into microscopes.
Bombsights
it occurs
to the young woman
moving from one
to another, peripherally
mesmerized
by the second hand, trees
flailing
dimly in windows.

3. On the Run

Winter hours, white
dune grass.
        Hidden
pine woods to the ocean—now what?

4. The Blackout: First Anniversary

It finds me in Port Authority, penniless,
seated at a bar unable to remember
how I came there (why is obvious).
Do you know this terror—not to remember?
I go to the men's room and look in the mirror,
look in his aggrieved and music-haunted eyes.
The mouth opens, but there are no words;
there are words, but the mouth will not open.
Tears form but cannot fall, fingers
gradually tightening at my throat . . .
Blood of his blood, flesh of his ghost—
the hand stretched toward me in the flames!
Do you?
I am worn out, I can't go on.

VOW

Love walk with me in the desert, the *blizzard* of Eden.

GENETICS

So many years I have been climbing and climbing the ladder invisibly minute; and when at last I come to that series of damaged or broken rungs, that will be it, so I'm informed: in that clear blue holy light, from a frightening height, finally I will get to look down—or simply let go and pass into a dark relief of falling, finally, forever. When all I ever wanted was to wander and stretch out and sleep for a while in those endless fields of irises. That, or to go down into the earth.

WITH THE GIFT OF A BRACELET

B.

The moon
a silver
sliver
(over
silver-spangled
river)—turquoise
evening all around

the beating wrist, dear
so often kissed left
under curve
of breast . . .
Oh lovely thinking
face, look
deeply

with your ears
(for me)
and listen into
with those blue eyes
(when mine are gone)
the deep smell of blue
night.

FROM A LINE BY REVERDY

To sit down at a table with Jesus
and eat a piece of fish
after his death, I don't think I could
bear it. But today I am following
in the blue stained-glass footsteps of a doctor who works with doomed
    children,
of the old poet, the rays in my eyes
walking to Heaven
which is not far—
a little face turns to the window
and it is there.

FATHER ROGER GOES FOR A WALK

It's September 13th again,
and the sun is shining.

This leafy largely vacant
rectory is just a place
for me to hang my head.

It's the last day of somebody's childhood.

And every day I'll try
to do one thing I like,
in memory of being happy.

A WORD FOR JOY

I am happy among children's eyes
I am very worried and happy
among the crazy and the hopeless
they recognize me, right away
I'm home
And there is nowhere I would rather be
alive or dead
than in this world
Inside this skull I hold and ponder
unending space expanding if I understand correctly
at an accelerating rate, meanwhile
housing perpetual births and disappearances of its numberless
        deafening nuclear furnaces unheard,
I consider the voices, identically soundless, in every
        mind, behind each face I pass
and as I've been instructed each morning
on rising I obliterate the print of my body
and am glad (the wind is blowing, it is written, adore
        the wind)
and am speechlessly grateful and glad and afraid
I don't mind saying that I am scared
to death of God: I am
afraid and blind and ignorant and naked and
I'll take it!
I have been happy here
among all the suffering eyes: why they were brought here
and exactly what it was they were expected
to take a good close look at,
I can't grasp it, but I am so very glad.

THE SONS: MARCH 2003

Soldiers again
resting under rare shade, which says
We are the trees. We are old, and tomorrow
we shall be older still, but
unlike you
we will still be here— . . .

This horror illusory if extremely persistent.
This Fourth World War with sticks and stones.
This month in anesthesia history.
This world perhaps a toy a child has tired of
and abandoned. Shrapnel struck the right ass cheek,

the hot jagged metal drove straight
on and passing under the bone
it entered the bladder—
he dropped, screaming, to his knees
and death was a red fog about him.

THE HAWK

Maybe in a million years
a better form of human
being will come, happier
and more intelligent. A few already
have infiltrated this world and lived
to very much regret it,
I suppose.
       Me,
I'd prefer to have come
in the form of that hawk, floating over
the mirroring fire
of Clearlake's
hill, my gold
skull filled with nothing
but God's will
the whole day through, instead
of these glinting voices incessantly
unerringly guiding me
to pursue
what makes me sick, and not to
what makes me glad. And yet
I am changing: this three-pound lump
of sentient meat electrified
by hope and terror has learned to hear
His silence like the sun,
and sought to change!
And friends
on earth at the same time

41

as me, listen: from the sound of those crickets
last night, René Char said
prenatal life
must have been sweet—
each voice perhaps also a star
in that night
from which
this time
we won't be
interrupted anymore—but
fellow monsters while we are still here, for one minute, think
about this: there is someone right now who is looking
to you, not Him, for whatever
love still exists.

THE HEAVEN

I lived as a monster, my only
hope is to die like a child.
In the otherwise vacant
and seemingly ceilingless

vastness of a snowlit Boston

church, a voice
said: I
can do that—

if you ask me, I will do it
for you.

THE READER

The mask was gone now, burned away
(from inside)
by God's gaze

There was no
I, there

was no he—
finally

there was no text, only
what the words stood for;
and then

what all things stand for.

III

EVERYONE'S ELEGY

Not all mankind will be cast into fire, though
quite a number of them were
during the decade preceding my
birth and no doubt even more will be
shortly. Why? This
no one knows—no one deserves this
and all deserve this, almost
all. But why
those particular ones, unremarkable, those
before and soon?
Only You know. And only You
know which group, the spared or murdered,
represent the doomed and which
the blessed—
the ones in the fire burned
clean of themselves, or those still remaining here
in this shocking place that more or less randomly vanished them. In
    any event,
blessed are the alone, for they shall be
befriended and blessed
the dead
for we shall live, perhaps
for the first time, still unborn
in this gorgeous hell of the material.
We will be inheriting soon
real reality, all
the peace of the universe:

unending night and the still hugely nameless
majority of the stars.

✳

D., 1959–2004

Until the sky gives up its
unendurable beauty of Bach heard by someone alone
in her room dying, I
wish for this sadness to leave
but it will never leave.
But I am also glad: I know that
at this very moment
your poor head is resting
on Christ's breast; I know you
are comfortably seated
at the Buddha's feet, listening
forever to his calm voice
and waiting
on me,
me
still failing
here, toward you, and
following
in the bodiless footsteps of God, most peripheral
and unlikely of followers,
keeping an eye on Him
from a distance and hoping to remain

among the unnoticed
in love.
       I am certain
you have now contributed your creature's
small light to the great peal of Light
still issuing from the beginning, and
rapidly traveling toward us from the end . . .

E. D. IN COMA

In her mind, in bare feet
she is walking among

April's first
cold
pubic violets, still

here, heaven-haunted
her eyes

and lips
closed:
Soon

so soon I'll be a part
of all that I
now merely
see

THE KNOWERS

Little bird bones come back
as a bird, as a bird
loudly singing
again
in the dead leaves
come back as green
leaves: only
we
don't return.

HELL

But if they were condemned to suffer
this unending torment, sooner or later
wouldn't they become the holy?

FOR FRANK STANFORD

The scheming and chattering
mind's abrupt sense
in the night of its being

surrounded by mind,
unendingly, starrily
dwarfed and encircled

by mind whose voice
is silence, utter
silence unequivocally

kind . . .
                    The first bird
talking to the last stars—

maybe it was you
who woke me today in the dark;
I know you're still around here somewhere.

I love you, therefore you are here.
For the first time in days I got dressed;
and I walked outside this morning,

and I saw a new heaven and a new earth.

FOR LARRY LEVIS

Among the dead I cannot find you.
Let me rest here a minute
beneath these six leaves, crippled
tree slightly taller than I am
in a Manhattan sidewalk like a streetlamp
in a forest where I'm lost.

FOR DONALD JUSTICE

There are happinesses gone forever
The days of receiving your letter
Or amidst blowing leaves, on the quiet
streets of small midwestern towns
late at night typewriter sounds.

ARKANSAS FIRST LIGHT

My life is so strange now, though I've come to love
this southern ghost place: the weather here
in January somewhat like the silver not-at-all-
cold light of Boston's March—and I hear there is snow

blowing over from Tulsa today, maybe
later this afternoon. My houseless life
here is so blessed, through scary hours
and of course long months of my Elizabethlessness:

I am very afraid but still know You
are taking care of me, and even live in hope
You will one day see fit to put into my mouth
words that will explain it all, floating before me in letters

of fire, the planet and her
sleeping face beginning
out of nothing to be made
visible once more.

ARKANSAS FIRST SNOW

What happens to me is not very important
(correction: not at all important)
but I will be sad never again

rather, it will be sad
never again
to read Blake's "The Sunflower," or Emily Dickinson's

"my departing blossoms . . . ,"
or to see your face.
I would like to go on doing that for some decades

and quietly studying the correspondences
of inner/outer worlds,
though I know they are one and the same now:

that emerald light shining far off in the distance

this afternoon as I was passing through
the empty park, snow beginning in earnest—
it can snow here!—I want to find out what it means;

I want to and I don't. I want to know
and I want the mystery,
                          both

but I doubt there will be enough time,
it's so far and so lovely from here.
Farther than ever.

ARKANSAS GOOD FRIDAY

I

Everyone knows what the cross means, or will
          before long

It is the body

It resembles the first stick-figure depictions
          of it found in caves (some
          with the heads of birds)

Depictions reproduced to this day by young children
          just learning to draw

Its aerodynamic properties ought to be obvious I suppose

to us,
the wingless

How many years we have been carrying it
And before too much longer it will reveal itself
the source of a forsakenness and agony
nobody would have dared foresee
I saw it
over twenty years ago

Every day as the darkness came down on New York
I went up to my father and saw

(More and more I meet him
in the mirror, it is his blood I have
to clean up if I shave— . . .)

And I was born just as I found him there

a little bald
toothless man
screaming,
not for long though
(I refer to Mother Morphine's left tit)

II

Now I'll tell you something you don't know, you hurt
by the past, just like me, crushed
by the future and blind
to the present,
blind
to the moment—

But there is nothing you don't know
I got up every morning here
a long way from home

and cried for ten minutes
then showered and dressed
and got back down to work
assisted, on occasion, by one or two magical mystery
        pills

III

I can tell you this
Who dwarfs my pain I cling to
the genuinely broken
and poor
And I cling to the Before
The spirit face
behind the face
yearning for light
the water and the light
And I am flowing back to the Before, the infinite
years which transpired while I was not
here, and did not know
I was not

here . . .
        I came just like you
from inconceivableness, the eternal
before-we-arrived, flowing

from God's mouth, and come here to say
"this world" and
                    "God," as if
they needed
names
            And what lies beyond is no doubt the beginning
I wouldn't know but I'm going
to find out
The what lies beyond
this loneliness and panic
I call dying, time, remorse, this cold
and purifying
fire, which hurts so much, which burns
away the world and all I was
who walked and breathed and spoke
how real it all seemed
for a few years, but I was always
immortal and will be
once more, when I return
to the infinite time
which elapsed before I was conceived;
when the heavenward face is burned away
and its scared eyes
and its tears
and its euphoria, which no one can imagine
(wrong: someone in love can imagine!)
And I have heard God's silence like the sun
now I long to return to it

no matter my infantile clinging
to this gorgeous material of such early wisteria and
        lilacs, the wind
in the redbud and light-giving new heart-shaped leaves
music visible if completely unheard, I'll return
The angel's going to raise his arms and sing that time is
        no more
nor tears: that numbered
sea of them is gone—
now there is a new sea, a new earth, a new sky—
and I will know what to say at the end: What end?
And I can add I found this world sufficiently miraculous
        for me, before I'm changed.

ALONE AND TALKING FUNNY

Car wreck outside Diamond, Arkansas
dreaming along
the Sunflower River

Under winter skies
        Under Lincoln's eyes—

Glass chapel like a ship perched on a pine ridge:

They think I have an accent
back in Boston
too,

no escape

Still I am that
once/now radiant
matter
that once was/is
the
Word

And the present
light shines through me too.

The final and ultimate act of compassion: return
        from peace to the place where you were tortured
        to death in order to comfort once more
        the frightened friends who'd deserted you, denying
        even having known you.

✡

Your friends slowly walking, eyes downcast, a
        little like Hiroshima's strange
        handful of unscathed survivors, the
        road out of Jerusalem—

You appeared among them, walked alongside them, asked
        them why they wept, yet for the longest
        time nobody recognized You, nobody knew
        who You might be

The road to Emmaus is this world

✡

We come out when the Watcher falls asleep

Counsels Whitman, spend time among powerful uneducated
        people

Living on nothing and dying of the world.

PETITION

Kneeling
at the foot of the universe

I ask

from this body
in confusion

and pain (a condition

which You
may recall)

Clothed now in light
clothed in abyss, at the prow
of the desert
killed
into everywhereness—

have mercy

Mercy on us all

ROSARY

Mother of space,
inner

virgin
with no one face—

See them flying to see you
be near you,

when you
are everywhere.

LINES WRITTEN IN THE DARK
ILLEGIBLE NEXT DAY

Apple alone in a bowl, and
then the sense-lit
apple
touched
(more on this presently)

And late at night I think I'm being followed: it
  is a bald child

in a white nightgown or wedding dress
which drags behind him
like the tides

The cat has no appointment
the bird no country
not a single
crumb

And did you notice the sky yesterday

It resembled a partially burnt sheet
of paper upon which remains
the fragment of a sentence I don't even want to think about

Cradled in his arms a bald doll he's pretending to nurse

Blood-colored shadow
of the rose: annunciation
to the crows

Tell you what, I will translate this for you

but only if they teach me how
to read

Words of rain

ON THE DEATH OF A CAT

In life, death
was nothing
to you: I am

willing to wager
my soul that it
simply never occurred

to your nightmareless
mind, while sleep
was everything

(see it raised
to an infinite
power and perfection)—no death

in you then, so now
how even less. Dear stealth
of innocence

licked polished
to an evil
luster, little

milk fang, whiskered
night
friend—

go.

FADING

Walking alone home from mass
one soft blue August morning I suddenly remember
in a dream, the night before, I met my mother
who informed me she had shrunk
another inch, "and maybe two."
We were standing inside a vast train station
with no ceiling. And I bent down to kiss her
goodbye, a white rose
as big as my head, nurse
appearing beside mein bed
and offering me her nipple whispering, If you scream
again you're going to get a shot. After the injection
I'm led by unseen hand into their vaulting
cafeteria of plastic scalpels
and saran-wrapped
genitalia
and commanded to vacuum
forever. Off in the distance—
sand blowing sideways—a solitary candle
burning in honor of my first
deathday. And if there is one
thing I simply cannot stand
to contemplate and one for which
the angels, I think, may desperately envy us
it's this knowledge of what it is like
to die: to see all things each day in light
of their certain vanishing, oh see them
with it
blaze!

THE POEM

In morning rain a dark
vast rustling mass of lilacs

summons me (greener
than the dreams of God), it

troubles me
awake, a

smemory—

DAWN WALKS IN BLUE AND DIAMONDS

Dawn walks in blue and diamonds
in robes of darkest grain
wind-parted

✳

Sleeping she looked
like a river
Like a river
at dawn,
silver

sliver
of moon, wind

in poplars, flickering

of a candle that grows
imperceptibly
taller as it burns

Manacled girl
naked
surrounded

by flames, gigantic

rose
of painless fire—

*

Now I have passed through
voice and fire
could I be cleansed
of all
desire,
I don't think so

Icon: cold gold telepathic eyes

*

Sacrament of metaphor, sacrament of matter

*

Aren't stars almost in your vicinity

It was only the barest beginning starward-
bound, only the March branches, only
the first gifts of the first awakening
waiting
forever
to be born . . .

*

Dawn walked in blue and diamonds.

PAYING

Oceanic whispers
of overhead leaves' apparitional
applause

rows of
granite
static

to my sundial
1953—
stone.

PRESCIENCE

We speak of Heaven who have not yet accomplished
even this, the holiness of things
precisely as they are, and never will!

Before death was I saw the shining wind.
To disappear, today's as good a time as any.
To surrender at last

to the vast current—
And look, even now there's still time.
Time for the glacial, cloud-paced

soundless music to unfold once more.
Time, inexhaustible wound, for
your unwitnessed and destitute coronation.

THE WALK

More malicious and frightening behavior
on the part of inanimate objects

I walked outside today, and the void was shining

Immortal and infinite
word
And I have heard
God's silence
like the sun

For the last time I stumbled
into a church
where no one was home, silently
screaming

Help me: I can't live

without You I don't want to live

I came in the midst of the world
and in the flesh I appeared to you
(I seemed to hear this, originless)
and I found you all
drunk and no one
did I find among you
thirsting

Staggered out again and took a look around
and suddenly noticed the others
each wearing that identical
expression, What is wrong with me—
What's going to happen
to me

And I heard again
the faceless voice
saying, How can you expect energy from above
when you continue to receive it
from below
and are content?

I   Am   Not   Content!

KINDNESS

There is a place where
even music is no longer
necessary
where I
am always
high

Where words are before somebody utters them
where leaves are before there are leaves
and where these friends
who never leave me
come from

No rest
for the
blessed

No poison envy
lushly clinging
and growing
around the
house twittering
darkening
everything

I will come to you memory shining

This body
is not me

SCALE

And this being
conscious
the chasm
between us and the universe finally
healed—

☆

O seasons,
endless
mansions

To live is to do evil

Drawings of grieving children
The dream capsules ready
And the tree of dark green pears that casts the shadow of
        a girl

Poor monster I must starve to stay alive . . .

Renunciant! Who sees you
Who notices
Who cares

Only the reverent are worthy of reverence

Seasons, mansions

A HAPPY THOUGHT

Assuming this is the last day of my life
(which might mean it is almost the first),
I'm struck blind but my blindness is bright.

Prepare for what's known here as death;
have no fear of that strange word forever.
Even I can see there's nothing there

to be afraid of: having already been
to forever I'm unable to recall
anything that scared me, there, or hurt.

What frightened me, apparently, and hurt
was being born. But I got over that
with no hard feelings. Dying, I imagine,

it will be the same deal, lonesomer maybe,
but surely no more shocking or prolonged—
It's dark as I recall, then bright, so bright.

LIVING TWICE

Like a young man's first
day in the city
where lords of words are known
to gather or labor on
in famous solitude

this day, its hallucinatory elation:

the hour's slowing down,
and ultimate cessation.
Home food and sleep's obviation
(and all that money it takes to be poor).

Awakened from need.
The miraculous the norm.
The minute's slowing down
and ultimate cessation,
that great gold wheel . . .

This day, and not
because I have
become that young dreamer
and certifiable
idiot once more,
on the contrary.

I know now
for sure

it will never be over,
no matter what I do, it
would never be enough—

Without horror
and at any shining
moment let it end then:
the second's slowing down
and final cessation!

Eyes filled with the great gold wheel of God's
eternal day.

DELIRIUM

I like to entertain
the wish everyone would forgive me
(even say nice things about me)
when I simply lie down
one day at long last
to give birth
to my no longer
being (here).
In a sense
only, that no longer
being. Because
where I am off to
is really not
so far: it is
in point of fact just
here, this
very same place, this
green and starry
world we loved
and dreaded. True
I'll be departing, but
I'm leaving here
to go here,
to arrive here
and
to be here, actually
be
what up until now I

merely daily
see. And you might even say
when the time comes
that "here" is what I am
at last, now. Where
else would I go, and
what else
would I be? I will be
seeing these (through your eyes) shining
leaves, I'll be touching
the world with your hand
signing our name
Oh go on for my sake
hear the music
we loved for me—
Remember me
to the sky
the wheat, the changing light, the clouds
the color of the incandescent distances
summer thunder from under that Maine hill, the
        strawberry
hill and those sea clouds, shimmering remoteness
the color of just barely audible
children's voices singing, the God-
did-not-allow-those-many-holocausts-
to-happen-we-did distances!
                                    See
the lightning for me, for me
station yourself in the storm and recall
that sometimes we needed the hurt
angry and passion-torn man
And remember me

awake, no longer
sleeping alone like a clenched fist
Remember the wine was already holy
(the glass of water's holy), remember
I will be walking beside you.

INTRODUCTION

How do you do. I am the broken
bird hidden in a grass-filled shoebox
and gradually nursed to death by some neglected child

I'm the crazy woman whose pet rat rides her left shoulder
drinking her tears.

      Wait a minute—
      allow me to regress.

      (See

there once was a weird little girl
whose weirdness was not all her fault;
for her shrink research father
kept locked in their vault-
like basement not one rat but scores of them, cage
stacked on cage of them, tiny
red green and yellow electrodes affixed
to their skulls.
I mean really.
I think I myself would turn into a strange
little mouse, forget
girl, if
brought up in that house:
she secretly possessed, you see,

to *that* truly fucked-up Dad's underworld,
her own bright silver key . . .)—

OK.

And I am her muteness,
                    the blue of her eyes

like the color of light filling up
vacant airliners' cabins at dawn,
                    and her night dreams, far happier and more real
than any psychiatrist's BMW life! Which
is as it should be: it is
the only rest and dark
the only
infinitely lonely
and cruel gift that psychosis has to offer.

I am her to learn
to bear
the beams of love,
what else

          Bells
through the leaves, I am here to endure the

bells tolling
underground

Like you a guest, a ghost here

Everything will be forgotten

And either I am too alone
or I am not
alone enough
to make each moment
holy

(No one bats 1000, friend
no one
bats 500)

And I have heard God's silence like the sun
and sought to change

Now
I'm just going to listen to the silence

till the Silence.

THE FIRE

Listen, I've light
in my eyes
and on my skin
the warmth of a star, so strange
is this
that I
can barely comprehend it:
I think
I'll lift my face to it, and then
I lift my face,
and don't even know how
this is done. And
everything alive
(and everything's
alive) is turning
into something else
as at the heart
of some annihilating
or is it creating
fire
that's burning, unseeably, always
burning at such speeds
as eyes cannot
detect, just try
to observe your own face
growing old
in the mirror, or
is it beginning
to be born?

WHY IS THE WINTER LIGHT

Why is the winter light
disturbing, and who
if anyone shares this impression?
If somebody enters the room
am I going to stop being afraid?
Why am I afraid
to go grocery shopping?
I suppose there is a pill for that, but
why? Surrounded by so vast
a cloud of witnesses
why do I feel this alone
in the first place? Is Heaven a place
and if so, will our poor
hairy speechless forebears—
all millions of years of them—
be there to greet us
if and when we arrive? The meek
shall inherit Auschwitz, too,
if they're not careful. Where do such obscenities
of thought originate? And are the words
we speak being mercilessly recorded, or
are we speaking the already written
premeditated words? Why
do I want to live
forever, and the next day
fervently wish I had died
when I was young? Why do I abruptly feel blessed?
And if (and it does) this city harbors

a single individual suffering
unendurably, am I
prepared to take his place?

*

Empty me of the bitterness and disappointment of being nothing but
      myself
Immerse me in the mystery of reality
Fill me with love for the *truly* afflicted
that hopeless love, if need be
make me one of them again—
Awaken me to the reality of this place
and from the longed-for or remembered place
And more than this, behind each face
induct, oh introduce me in-
to the halting disturbed ungrammatical soundless
words of others' thoughts
not the drivel coming out of our mouths
Blot me out, fill me with nothing but consciousness
of the holiness, the meaning
of these unseeable, all
these unvisitable worlds which surround me:
others' actual thoughts—everything
I can't perceive yet
know

know it is there.

THE NEXT HOME

1. Moving In

With half a mind
to blow my brains out, half
to get real high
and half
to finish
this: look
my very own
unfurnished bare bulb–lit
interior,
        where
I will unwitnessed
kill someone
(all I know
is that someone named
Franz Wright has
ruined me) or
live—

2. Missed

And I did, I put the bullet in
my head,
I thought

(A single lead
antidepressant and all
would be cured)

Yet something, apparently,
                    lightly
brushed the thing away;

the way my mother might a fly
hovering about the temple
of a sleeping child.

3. Dreamt Final Verse of a Song (Melody Lost)

It was raining and we ducked into a movie:
It was a triple feature and we fell asleep.
And when we woke the preacher
Was raving from the velvet pulpit;
And many had been born,
And the dead filled their bags by the score.
And the children were up in the balcony playing
        with their drugs and Tonkas.

4. 5:45 a.m.

In appearance it is the same sky, the same
        swaying blue
treetops I noticed

93

at six months of age, but
these days I get the feeling
I really am seeing them,
lilac-blue treetops,
for the final time;
and have to say their being
there and my own
being perceiving them
here
seems to me now as identically
and inexpressibly strange
as it did then, I suppose,
in my elderly
infancy—I still can't talk,
I still can't
tell anyone.

5. God Here

The uninterruptible
voice, the
silence I now call
my only
friend

Who says

right about now you might want to stop playing
mad chemist with your brain: return to Me

and I will return

6. Goodbye to a Friend with No Mother Tongue

But which language did you dream in

In what language
did you cry

Which one
did you fly in . . .

In what words can we possibly die

Forget our names and close our eyes?

IV

LOVE

While they were considering whether to stone her—
and why not?—he knelt
and with his finger wrote
something in the dust. We are
as you know made from
dust, and the unknown
word
was, therefore, and is
and forever will be
written in our flesh
in gray folds of
memory's
flesh. *En*
archê ên ho logos:

FIVE OCTOBERS (ON OUR ANNIVERSARY)

Was this torture
or life-saving surgery?
Hard to tell. Would I see you again (apparitional
hand extended, shining, to the drowning)
or had I been scheduled
irrevocably
for amputation?

I let it ring and ring: no answer

and how could there be
when at that very moment you were standing at my door
about to knock, prepared
for anything, even
a life spent spoon-feeding this mute
strange broken man.

Had our parts been reversed, my only
hope is this: I
would have done unto you
as you—impossibly—did
to
and for me

and see
how the limbs once thought dead bloomed again
by your mercy
and unalterable (never

mind undeserved)
love.

So I would take my stand to watch
with you, I would station myself
in the storm and, if not struck down, listen
to see
one last time
what was going to be said to me
and what I would answer—

No publication, no prizes, no
young misinformed
adulation, no nothing
but this unnoticed glory, just to work
once more
to save me: the only
rest and dark the gift, the voice unbidden
brings, it would be
mine again now you were
mine again, Beth.

Five Octobers later

I am made of light and I am spreading out
into an infinite
black space until I am "gone"—
we will never be gone, not

the blessed, the born, everyone—

like every grass blade, sand grain, sun

we change not
die,

we will never not be here
(you prove this, child's face shining through
the grieving ageing face
of you,
mercy in person) . . .

Love, I was having such dawn thoughts
exultant due to you, when
we looked over and saw them, not one

but two foxes ten yards from us, maybe, just staring.
They were seated, the way cats sometimes do,
on their butts, however erect and quite curious.

Then they glanced at each other
and slipped away side by side
into the fox-colored trees, love

let us die, as we must, let us die
just like that!

Just like that, never die—

WAKE

I saw my friend the other day
we were all attending his wake
and he was the only one there
who looked like he was well
Somehow he'd gotten well
He looked like he was doing fine There
Everyone else in the room looked just awful

Strange how little say I had in all I said

That's what his relaxed and now youthful face seemed
just about to say
anyway those were the words
that abruptly appeared in my head

And: I have heard God's silence like the sun
and longed to
change

And one way or another I was going to
And if I could not manage to do it, it would be done
to me

You can't choose
where you come from

But looking down into the white face I knew
one day I would have to
choose

Heaven

Only Your friends can
render, here, visible
the kingdom
that bright glory

Look my friend is there

THE BELOVED ILLUSORY

At some point, forever, I crossed
into a state where my words
became more real than I am (even to me)
Is that a good thing
or a bad thing, I
have absolutely no idea
but every day I thank God for this consciousness
that neither
one is real—

I greet our star
each day with words
of immeasurably mortal breath
to this effect: the sun
itself will die

At which I find my prison
mysteriously open
unattended
I am free
and not alone
already One

In sleep I still tend to decay
back into myself
back into my terror and ignorance, but once awake

I can suddenly see the whole universe
like an apple I hold in my hand!

And while we're at it
let me state for the record I have no mind
to lose. Now
the sky is my mind.

The beginning beckons
I'm tired of just talking about it

The book almost done, a dark entertainment
for others
while they wait
(our blessedness)
to disappear.

Redisappear.

LANGUAGE MY COUNTRY

Language: my country
where night
rhymes with light, death

                    with breath—

And from childhood on the gift
of seeing world the way
the dying see

it: things shining

in the light of their imminent disappearance.

EXAMPLE

And the Ariadne artery—

NEBRASKA BLIZZARD

1974

We were about to make Omaha
halfway through
the winter.
Someone who is dead now
handed me a joint.

So we should have light if
required someone else
bought a little flashlight
at a store just off the highway.

It was getting dark, starting to snow.
60,000 years ago You opened my lips . . .

I stood at the side of a beckoning
wheat field
and tried to take a leak.
I spent a long minute then
checking my eyes in the rearview.

Eyes cruel with pain—
they looked just like his
reflected in a knife: my brother,
the death of the body.
He at least was never,

never scared.

TWO POEMS

1. After Issa

Snow falling
on my blanket: even this
issuing from the clean hand.

2. After Celan

Dull sun
across a black gray desolation.
A tree-
high thought embracing
this dirty shade of light: there are
still songs
to sing past
man.

THE INSANE

They've fallen silent now, because the wall that separates
the mental from the concrete life is gone;
and there are too few articulate minutes
in their hour to say what they go through.

Suddenly, however, and often late at night,
they get well.
The hands lie among actual things,
the heart remembers how to pray,
and the eyes gaze down, unaghast,

into the clarity—no longer even hoped for—
of a garden in the quiet square.
A few can recall how it really appears
when they return to their own strangeness forever.

Translated from the German of Rainer Maria Rilke

WHO SAID THAT

Just before waking I heard
quite distinctly my father alive
again alive
which means as usual

quoting from memory unheard-
of verses which signified
apparently I was fifteen once
more and this is what the dear voice

said (voice as vivid to this day to me
as any living voice): *Our flies*
know a few songs
they learned them

from the flies in Norway
who are the divinities
of the snow

who said that?

PREPARATIONS

When I look at the bare fields in winter, the sunflowers are there.

When I gaze at the sunflowers I see the scarred snowy fields.

This is how you can tell you are ready to leave

this beautiful and deadly place,
depart

and return there,
                    annihilated,
healed.

                    While there is time

I call to mind Your constant unrequited
and preemptive forgiveness.

And remember You are not
and never were the object
of my thought,
my prayer,
my words
            but rather *I*
was the object of Yours!

And I think I'm beginning to learn finally
what everything has been trying to teach me

just recently
again, and
for the past fifty years of forever:
total love for You—the mysterious gift of my life—
truly felt at each instant
and every day
of deepest recollection,
grace-filled apprehension, it *would*
dispel all fear, as well
as the love that requires
a response—
from others, other
ghosts (or
even
You!)

And I have always failed, yet
always know IT was there—this utter love—
And so am ready with the speechless
universe all word
my company,
my light,
my sunflower. Dark morning thoughts— . . .

POET'S ROOM IN A MUSEUM

A white sheet
of paper upon
which the words
The undecided light or

It's snowing
in the past appear
and vanish one
by one

Three lbs. of sentient meat
afloat
inside a big pickle jar

saying, Where did I come from
Where
are my dead friends

White sheet upon which the following—

Poem may be defined as the voice of some human being happier and more intelli-
gent than anyone who exists

Poem is not composed in states of exaltation: most that are, in fact, result in total
doggerel and, frankly, insufferable puke. True poem might be defined as the most
successful inducer (in reader and startled author alike) of that hopelessly longed-
for state of exaltation

Poem in other words may or may not result from inspiration but must (in reader and author alike) produce it—

Poem should create the impression of a single correctly spelled word

No poem without its dark punch line, wherever it may occur, the anti-punch line

Lastly poem should always be completely clear, completely concrete and completely inexplicable, like reality itself; poem's purpose is to transcend words—to transcend mere words by pointing to reality, encountering and contributing to reality, and finally joining it, just as our purpose is to finally die, entering earth, water or fire to rejoin what has heretofore only been perceived, enjoyed, suffered. It will if successful allow one who possesses a gift for gazing with stillness and emptiness into it to pass, for a moment, into the eternal future and origin, no longer in the world but an inseparable element of it, and so forth

—appears and vanishes

one word
at
a
time . . .

LESSON

Because what is outer is inner
there is no outer
there is no inner—
I am trying to get this straight
And what the long sentence
assembled
by cemetery sparrows said
before my presence
arrived
dispersing them in its brief
wake, oh
wordless endless.

THE CHOICE

When you look at the sky, when you look at the stars, God is not
there.

Someone in Hell is sitting beside you on the train.
Somebody burning unnoticed walks past in the street.

Sailors in snow—

God can do what is impossible, but
God can only do what is impossible.

Sad incurable gift.

WRONG

After you were dead, I thought

nothing really terrible can ever happen now.

You've been having a few words with me on this
        subject

today, I stand corrected
and appalled—

       though on one point
more firmly than ever rooted, one
in which you cannot but remain where you are,
buried,

    answerless:

never again can I stab you in the heart.

MONTH SIX

I feel like I'm lost in a desert with two suns, one rising
while the other goes down,
how about you?

I feel like I'm standing in somebody's dorm room
my book on the desk, open
to this page: November

light, bare

infectious shadows
moving on the pillow

some sort of distant whale song
through the glass
silently bending the pines

It's 1974—
remember, before
cocaine became addictive—

Strange years that have crossed our country

And those were the wrong roses for John Lennon, don't
you think

I speak of my daughter the wind with its long graying
hair

and I'm not even born, there

where summer ends,
                    crucified
to a barn door
in the northern Ohio of sleep

still preparing

to recite my first telephone number
and marry the snow.

TO THE SUN, TO THE RISEN

For now you are still
just a word, but
the time is not far
when you will namelessly
unperceived
shine once
again

So the visionary is whatever is
self-evident
e.g.

I am voyaging around the sun for now

Return me to, return
to me

the still gold-lit
place
of Your peace

still gold-lit

space

I have quieted my soul like a weaned child

And permit my small translation
to nothing at last

DOCTRINE

Dear animal

form we are
entering the
world

of the spirit, of the way

the universe appeared when we weren't there.

Clear radiant awareness
without an object (and
without a subject) . . .

The sun in space, the sun

imagined and the word
sun

on this page:

twelve neocortex-haloed
apes in a circle
inventing

the zero

at each moment, practicing

the presence of God.

EVENT HORIZON

Children of Chernobyl
on a field trip to the woods
of Germany, where my wife meets them

on a path and one approaches,
takes her hand in his
six-fingered hand, and whispers

solche schöne Hände—
How many people can say that
for a minute they knew why they'd lived?

STRANGER'S STUDY: BERLIN

Over gates
of Auschwitz: the satanically
sarcastic take

on Christ's "The truth
will set you free" (*"Wahrheit
macht frei"*): *"Arbeit
macht frei"* . . . I

have never once heard
anybody comment
on this,
strange.

My host's
a ghost. (Well,
she
is me.)

The chair's
a stair
to
nowhere.

With all my
might I

switched off
the light:

dark's
my light;
closed eyes
my sight.

My genre,
silence—
the after-
science.

PARTING WORD

As for me
I have no mind
to lose anymore, I am through
with all that—
the sky is my mind
today. (And

it always is
and always was

today.) Blue,
        her color
sorrowing over us . . .

Does it flow out of or into us, seeing?

Unseen ray of perception the face beams
at things, or
face on which things shine!
I am so glad

that I no longer know,
no longer
care.
And one more thing:

the future?
Never

been there.

THE POEM

Abject silence

and the hours

of hesitation
fear-induced
imbecility

in this attempt to speak to
speak for
Whom?
        To

make this little
changeless
thing.

OCTOBER

Crows' shadows flocked to the moon;
I was drinking a glass of water, or
smoking a cigarette in a dream.

I was talking to you on the telephone, but
did I wake or sleep? And
what about this wide-spread sentient

chauvinism—any thoughts
on that? So much depends
on who you are when you are dead . . .

A hand is the glove, in any event,
a human face the mask
of some being no one can see.

On that I think we can agree.

ELEGY: THE BOY

The instant we learned how not to cry
suggested the great Leonard Michaels
somebody else began

growing inside us, a lengthening
shade, nameless
mourner:

            the one
to whom from that point on
we'd delegate all pain,

but I have woken up from him.
Traveling, each one alone, toward
the beginning's

finster Finisterre—

toward the before it all happened,
the Reunion;
the forgiving.

THE QUESTION

It is pondering
me again

And the great ineluctably altering cloud
of the brain passing, passing away, slowly
polishing the peaks
(and just leave it alone
let it be
what it is: a bright
yet always needful
of a good dusting
little mirror, one
nevertheless
radiantly aware—without need
of object *or* subject—
aware,
      its own
impossibility and sweetness) . . .
polishing and polishing
that lovely high
unvisited and evidently
never to be
summited place

as it magestically slowly sails on

OHIO SUNFLOWERFIELD

Hiddenly, one minute
each one believes
death to be
an unforeseen
catastrophe
only occurring
elsewhere, to
everyone else,
and the next
minute a personal
doom to which he
alone is condemned—

What's wrong with the truth, so profoundly consoling and
        perfect?

A SUCCESSFUL DAY (FILL IN THE BLANK)

It has been given back, all I was denied and all
I then took over denying myself for more than thirty years—
a cheerful self-confident trust that I am at home in this
　　　　　universe,
and pity for the afflicted (because as one of the afflicted
I could pity and identify with no one but myself).

I would like to give my life
the sad and awful simplicity
of an early weekday mass with
a handful of most lonely humans in attendance.

What have I ever gained by (1) answering the telephone
(2) reading the newspaper
(3)

This morning I had supper with the infinite.
Dorothy Wordsworth wrote: *a rainy day,*

I made a shoe.

AFTER

I was,
still carrying darkness
into bright day, and light
into the depths
singing

through the din of sheep bleating
with throats cut
"Life, my life"

Singing
things seen
in the radiance
of my imminent disappearance

You don't build your house on a bridge

And so much ecstasy, how could I tell you

Those were the days all right
And they will surely come again
Oh, not for me—
but they will come.

THE PROCESS

Unbidden it comes, without warning, and completely undeserved:
a mounting hallucinogenic
tranquility accompanied

by a slowing and, finally, total cessation of
time in which I freely and lucidly
move, make tea and so forth, muttering

words alone to myself, in a happiness
which for reasons best known to Yourself I was blessed with
from childhood on. And with alongside it

the long black killing years
of its infrequency or absence, that
can always come again,

according to Your will.
But when it does, this time
I will not whine, I will obey

and be
(forever)
still.

ADMISSION

Like much-loved music things
(when I am at my gladdest)
physical objects themselves
appear to represent
something I can't see
(not yet)—
something
I cannot recall or imagine
yet whose presence I clearly perceive
the way perhaps the born blind do
the sun.
Like words
most masterfully uttered
these concrete things stand for
invisible things, while
remaining themselves,
their dear selves, without which
I just can't imagine my life;
I believe in a higher unseeable
life, inconceivable
light
of which light is mere shadow, and yet
already, at times, and with desolation
with bereftness no words can express, miss this light
of the earth, this bright life
I yesterday only began to love, to understand.

UNDER THE LAMP, OUT OF THE DEPTHS

As I sat alone retouching
poem's emerging face

for no reason it happened
I turned my head

and saw you lying in my bed
your blue

blue eyes wide open
intensely watching me

in the innocence of God
in the morning light—

SCRIBBLED TESTAMENT

I stand before you
here, some hairy
primate's fall from grace—
one of the patients of God,
one of the orphans of light.

Having read the great books
of this world, only
to completely forget them again;
having learned how to speak
this language only

(darken it up a bit will you)
to translate my heart for you
from the original
silence;
in the end, I was

simply borrowing it
from its inventors
the dead and the brilliant
unborn,
forgive me.

I AM LISTENING

I could not get out of bed
for sixteen years a day.
I could not
rouse myself to take a bath. How
resubmerge this broken
body in the waters of electrocution—
how return, redescend
to find it a book
or wash its bruised clothes
the basement stairs
to the site of
its hanging, a failure
even at that?

Delivered, I'm still stung by my abandonment
of those unmeetable
ones who still live there
in Hell.

Tell me.

Could I be allowed
with them
a quiet word?

And what
might that word be?

There must be a way: how
assure them, remind them
they too come from the light at the beginning of time.

Proved faithless, still I wait.

NOTES

"Transformation" is dedicated to my friend Heidi Arnold.

✳

"The Truth Will Set You Free" is dedicated to Daria Donnelly.

✳

"Alder Street" is for Trish.

✳

The final verse of "Text & Commentary" is based on a line by César Vallejo.

✳

My wife, Elizabeth, collaborated with me in the writing of "On the Death of a Cat" and "I Am Listening."

✳

The italicized passage in "The Walk" is taken more or less verbatim from the Oxyrhynchus Papyrus, discovered in 1897 by B. P. Grenfell and A. S. Hunt in the course of their excavations at the site of the ancient city of Oxyrhynchus (at the modern Behnesa in central Egypt). The papyrus was written about the year A.D. 200 and contains seven sayings, all introduced by the words "Jesus says." That is to say, it contains a collection of extracanonical sayings of Jesus—not a continuous discourse, but excerpts from an unknown gospel.

✳

The Issa version in "Two Poems" is supposed to be the last poem the elderly haiku master composed, apparently after being carried by stretcher from his burning house during a snowstorm.

✳

The author of the italicized passage in "Who Said That" is, of course, Apollinaire.

✳

I would like to thank my friends Ilana Kurshan and Rosamond Coss for introducing me to the writings of Abraham Joshua Heschel and Thich Nhat Hanh, constant sources of illumination and companionship during the composition of this book.

ACKNOWLEDGMENTS

Some of these poems originally appeared in the following journals:

Agni Review: "Two Poems: After Celan"

Bat City Review: "Kindness" and "October"

Boston College Magazine: "Admission"

Colorado Review: "Emperor of Antarctica"

Daedalus (American Academy of Arts & Sciences): "The Choice" and "Lesson"

Field: "The Knowers," "A Happy Thought," "For Donald Justice," "Lines Written in the Dark Illegible Next Day," "Scribbled Testament," "Publication Date," "Sitting Up Late with My Father, 1977," and "Did This Ever Happen to You"

Five Points: "Petition" and "Woods Hole Ferry"

Fugue: "Introduction," "The Heaven," "Everyone's Elegy," "Wake," "Poet's Room in a Museum," and "Ohio Sunflowerfield"

Image: "Arkansas Good Friday" and "Text & Commentary"

LIT: "Doctrine," "The Reader," "Arkansas First Light," "Arkansas First Snow," "To the Sun, to the Risen," and "Parting Word"

Literary Imagination: "The Two"

Nebraska Review: "Poem in Two Parts," "Alder Street," "Vow," "Genetics," "With the Gift of a Bracelet," "From a Line by Reverdy," "Father Roger Goes for a Walk," "A Word for Joy," "The Sons: March 2003," "The Hawk," "Dawn Walks in Blue and Diamonds," and "Paying"

New York Quarterly: "Child Playing," "The Next Home," "For Larry Levis," "Elegy: The Boy," "Language My Country," and "Event Horizon"

Passport: "The Truth Will Set You Free"

Salmagundi: "Nebraska Blizzard," "Wrong," "A Successful Day (Fill in the Blank)," "The Fire," and "Month Six"

Slope: "Transformation," "From the Past," and "Progress"

Typo: "For Frank Stanford"

Vallum: "I Am Listening," "Five Octobers (On Our Anniversary)," "Why Is the Winter Light," and "Living Twice"

Special thanks to the editors of *The New Yorker* where the following poems originally appeared: "East Boston, 1996," "On the Death of a Cat," "Prescience," "The Visiting," "Four Poems of Youth," and "E. D. in Coma."

"The Visiting" also appeared in *Best American Spiritual Writings 2004* (Houghton Mifflin).

"Publication Date" also appeared in *180 More: Extraordinary Poems for Every Day* (Random House, 2005).

"Alone and Talking Funny," "The Poem," and "A Question" also appeared in *Härter.*

"On the Death of a Cat" also appeared in *The Great Cat: Poems About Cats* in the Pocket Poets Series of the Everyman's Library (Random House, 2005).

"Prescience" was also printed as a broadside by the Poetry Center of Chicago, and appeared in *Best American Spiritual Writings 2005* (Houghton Mifflin).

"The Fire" also appeared in the *Cúirt International Poetry Festival Annual,* 2005.

A NOTE ABOUT THE AUTHOR

Franz Wright was born in Vienna in 1953 and grew up in the North-
west, the Midwest, and Northern California. His most recent works
include *Ill Lit: Selected & New Poems*, *The Beforelife* (a finalist for the
Pulitzer Prize), and *Walking to Martha's Vineyard* (which won the Pulitzer
Prize for poetry). He has been the recipient of two National Endow-
ment for the Arts grants, a Guggenheim Fellowship, a Whiting Fel-
lowship, and the PEN/Voelcker Prize, among other honors. He lives
in Waltham, Massachusetts, with his wife, the translator and writer
Elizabeth Oehlkers Wright.

A NOTE ON THE TYPE

The text of this book was set in Centaur, the only typeface designed by Bruce Rogers (1870–1957), the well-known American book designer. A celebrated penman, Rogers based his design on the roman face cut by Nicolas Jenson in 1470 for his *Eusebius*. Jenson's roman surpassed all of its forerunners and even today, in modern recuttings, remains one of the most popular and attractive of all typefaces.

The italic used to accompany Centaur is Arrighi, designed by another American, Frederic Warde, and based on the chancery face used by Lodovico degli Arrighi in 1524.

Composed by Stratford Publishing Services,
Brattleboro, Vermont
Printed and bound by United Book Press,
Baltimore, Maryland
Designed by Virginia Tan